CRUCIAL CONVERSATIONS

THE RIGHT WAY

2 Manuscripts in 1 Book, Including: How to Talk to People and How to Influence People

Dean Mack

More by Dean Mack

Discover all books from the Social Skills Best Seller Series by Dean Mack at:

bit.ly/dean-mack

Book 1: *How to Flirt*

Book 2: *How to Start a Conversation*

Book 3: *How to Talk to People*

Book 4: *How to Ask Questions*

Book 5: *How to Be Funny*

Book 6: *How to Influence People*

Book 7: *How to Attract Men*

Book 8: *How to Attract Women*

Themed book bundles available at discounted prices:

bit.ly/dean-mack

Table of Contents

BOOK 1: HOW TO TALK TO PEOPLE 5

BOOK 2: HOW TO INFLUENCE PEOPLE........................... 62

HOW TO
TALK TO PEOPLE
THE RIGHT WAY

The Only 7 Steps You Need to Master
Conversation Skills, Effective Communication
and Conversation Tactics Today

DEAN MACK

BOOK 1: HOW TO TALK TO PEOPLE

THE RIGHT WAY

The Only 7 Steps You Need to Master Conversation Skills, Effective Communication and Conversation Tactics Today

Dean Mack

Respective authors own all copyrights not held by the publisher.

The information herein is offered for informational purposes solely, and is universal as so. The presentation of the information is without contract or any type of guarantee assurance.

The trademarks that are used are without any consent, and the publication of the trademark is without permission or backing by the trademark owner. All trademarks and brands within this book are for clarifying purposes only and are the owned by the owners themselves, not affiliated with this document.

Table of Contents

Introduction 9

Chapter 1: The Basics 11

Chapter 2: The 7 Steps 20

Chapter 3: Best Practices 44

Conclusion..58

Introduction

Learning how to talk effectively is important. Whether you want it or not, there is a constant flow of communication that happens everywhere. In fact, even if you choose not to talk, you still communicate a message to those around you. In the world today, communication remains as important as it has always been thousands of years ago. After all, before robots and computers can do their job, there must first be human interaction — and the best way to interact with another human being is by using effective communication techniques.

The following chapters will teach you everything that you need to know about mastering the art of talking to people and communicating effectively.

Chapter 1 lays down the basics, so that you will have a strong foundation and understanding of what effective communication is all about.

Chapter 2 reveals the 7 steps that you need to master the art of talking to people. This part of the book reveals what you need to learn to become a highly-effective communicator.

Chapter 3 discusses the best practices of effective communication. Learn additional tips and tricks that can further develop your communication skills.

May this book be your guiding light to success and a happier life.

Chapter 1: The Basics

What is effective communication?

Being able to communicate is a vital element of humanity. The history of communication can be traced back to the time when warriors would form a circle around a bonfire and exchange stories with one another. Today, there are so many ways and means to communicate: You can send a text message, write an email, make a phone call, and others. Still, nothing beats face-to-face communication as being the most personal and effective manner of talking with another human being.

There are many definitions of what communication is. According to Merriam Webster's Dictionary, communication is "the act or process of using words, sounds, signs, or behaviors to express or exchange information or to express your ideas, thoughts, feelings, etc., to someone else." Simply put, communication is about expressing yourself to another person. It is worth noting that many people know how to communicate — even a baby communicates with her parents. However, only a few know how to communicate effectively, in a way that people will really hear and understand what you are trying to express. This book is about *effective* communication, which is about being able to communicate your thoughts, feelings, and ideas, clearly and more effectively. This is about having a real conversation with another human being.

Is it important to learn effective communication? This is a legitimate question. After all, most people do not know how to communicate effectively and merely say whatever ideas they may have in mind, so why would anyone bother to learn effective communication? Of course, you are free to decide whether or not you want to take the effort to learn how to talk effectively. You can stay the way that you are right now, but you can also improve your communication skills and see the significant and positive difference that it can do to your life.

People who know how to communicate effectively tend to be more successful in life. They are also the ones who establish a good network of connections. This is because human beings like people who communicate clearly and effectively. Take note that this is not just about having a conversation, but effective communication also means making the other person feel good about having a conversation with you. As you can see, true effective communication is not just about expressing your thoughts and ideas to another. It goes beyond the simple definition of what communication is all about and also takes into consideration the whole communication process, as well as the entire experience of having a conversation.

Have you noticed people who seem to be able to command a whole audience just by talking? How about people who are able to carry on a conversation for hours yet still capture the attention and interest of his audience? These people are the ones who communicate effectively. Of course, effective communication does not just work before a crowd of people. It also works powerfully in a one-on-one conversation setup. These days, many people have the habit of communicating; however, they do not do so effectively. In fact, many people are poor communicators and barely manage to get a message across clearly. If you learn and practice the techniques in this book that will turn you into a real effective communicator, then you can set yourself apart and have your own brand. People will like talking with you. In fact, they will like you as a person. This, of course, can open lots of doors of opportunity. Learning to communicate effectively can change your life, as well as the life of the people you talk to. It simply has its own magic that can create a positive impact.

The communication process

The communication process refers to a process whereby two or more people exchange information. Take note that it is an *exchange* of information and not just about sending information to another. Hence, it is a two-way process where the parties take turns to talk and listen to each other.

The communication process has 6 parts or elements. Let us take a look at them one by one:

➢ Sender

The sender is the one that starts the communication process. The sender is also referred to as the *source*. The sender has an information, thought, or idea, or even an emotion that he would like to share to another. In order to do this, he will have to encode the message in a form that will be understood by another, and then transmit the message.

➢ Receiver

Once the message of a sender is transmitted, it is directed to a receiver, or the person to whom the sender is talking to and to whom he wishes to convey the said information. Once the receiver receives the message coming from the sender, he will then have to decode it. This is the reason why the language used by the sender should be something that the receiver understands so that he (the receiver) will easily be able to decode the message and understand what the sender is trying to express.

➢ Message

Obviously, this refers to the information that the sender wants to communicate to the receiver. If you combine the sender, receiver, and the message, altogether, then you have the most basic elements of a communication process. However, the process does not really end there.

> Medium

The medium is also referred to as the *channel*. It simply refers to the means that the sender uses to send his message. For example, a text message can be sent using a mobile phone as the medium.

> Feedback

At the basic level a communication is complete once the sender is able to transmit his message and the said message is receiver by the receiver. However, it is not the end of the process. Once the receiver has received the message, he then responds to the sender. This is to indicate that he has received and understood the message. A feedback usually keeps the communication process active and on-going. It can be verbally made or even in writing. It can even be expressed through one's actions.

> Other factors

The communication process is also subject to other elements that may affect how the information is sent, received, and understood:

Noise - A noise usually comes in the form of interference that makes the information difficult to be understood. It can refer to the actual noise in the environment which makes it hard for the receiver to even hear the voice of the sender, or it can also refer to the static interference when communication over the phone. Anything that hinders the communication process may be considered a noise.

Context - The context by which something is transmitted can affect how the other person would understand it. This, of course, can affect the quality of the exchange of information. This may have some social and cultural aspect into it. Hence, before you transmit any message, be sure to do so in the right context in order to avoid misunderstanding. For example, to the Chinese, calling them as *intsik*, which is just another term for *Chinese*, is considered insulting. Hence, when you are talking with a Chinese person, do not include the word *intsik* when you transmit a message; otherwise, the receiver might feel insulted even if you are saying something pleasant.

Time element - Time can also be considered another factor. This refers to the time when the receiver gets to receive or read the message transmitted by the sender. This normally applies in cases where you are not engaged in a face-to-face conversation. For example, when you communicate via email or text messaging. You cannot always be sure that the receiver will be able to get your message immediately after you send it.

It is worth noting that effective communication means so much more than knowing the communication process. Being aware of this process is only good in order to help you understand how a communication normally takes place, but being a truly effective communicator means so much more than knowing how the process works. This, however, can give you a good idea on how you can communicate more effectively.

Is it for you?

Many people are aware of the term *effective communication*, but only a few are truly able to communicate effectively. So, is it for you? The good news is that effective communication is for everyone. This is because anyone can learn it. However, just like anything that is worth learning, you will need to dedicate your time and efforts to it. This is not something that you can just learn overnight. It takes practice and commitment to become an effective communicator, but it is nevertheless learnable and doable.

The following chapters will walk you through the 7 steps that will turn you into an effective communicator. If you stick to these steps and practice them continuously, then you will soon be able to learn and even master the art of effective communication. If you are a complete beginner who is just starting out, then do not expect to be able to master the following steps quickly and easily. But, if you persist in your practice, then these steps will get easier over time. Soon, they will become second nature to you. Allow these steps to become a part of you, and you will be able to do them smoothly and naturally.

So, is effective communication for you? The answer is *yes*, and it is well within your reach. The secrets to learning the art of effective communication and conversation are revealed in the pages of this book. Just keep your determination strong, never stop learning, and keep on practicing. This book will give you the knowledge that you need; it is up to you to turn it into actual practice.

Why would anyone want to learn how to talk to people effectively? If you stop for a while and notice what is going on around you, it is easy to recognize that the "machinery" of how the world works is mainly based on how people talk with one another. Gone are the days when swords and steel had to do the talking. In the modern world, people just talk to set things in motion. Whether you are in a workplace environment, in school, or even just in the comfort of your home, it is talking with one another that connects people. It is also how ideas, feelings, and thoughts are usually expressed. Hence, if you learn how to talk to people effectively, then just imagine the benefits that you can enjoy. You will be able to express your ideas more accurately; you can even influence people with your words; you can be a better negotiator; you can make people open up to you; you can build good relationships with people, and so much more. The possibilities become limitless. This is because you will be able to talk and connect with people on a deeper level. And, as you may already know, once you establish this kind of connection with people, then chances are that you can work together mutually and more effectively. Talking effectively with people is probably one of the best things to experience in life, and it can also open lots of opportunities for you.

Chapter 2: The 7 Steps

#1 Prepare

Preparation can go a long way. In fact, if you have enough preparation, then you could almost guarantee being able to talk effectively. But, how do you prepare? This is where the problem usually is. Many people know the importance of doing preparation, but only a few are able to do *sufficient* preparation.

If you know that you will be talking with someone, the first step that you should do is to prepare for the meeting. Know as much about the person whom you will be talking to. Find out about his interests, if possible. Although communication is about voicing out your thoughts and ideas, an important part of effective communication is to know about the other person. This should be part of your preparation. This is like preparing for a date. This will ensure that you can keep the other person interested in conversing with you. By talking about the other person's interest, you can make the other person happy talking with you. A common mistake made by beginners is to prepare only for the things that they want to say, without making any preparation for meeting the other person. Take note that you are dealing with another human being and not just someone who will listen and receive whatever you want to say.

There are no hard and fast rules on how you should prepare. The manner and amount of preparation that you need will depend on the circumstances of the situation. So, for example, you will be meeting with a business tycoon. Find out and research what his business is all about. If he is engaged in the stock market, then try to learn interesting things about the stock market. Also learn the current trend and happenings in the stock market. One way to communicate effectively is to talk about something that the other person is interested in.

Another part of your preparation is to expect the topics and subtopics that will be brought up during the actual meeting. It is important for you to have a good understanding of the subject matter so that you can give insightful and meaningful opinions. If you do not have a good grasp of the subject matter, then it will be hard to communicate anything worthwhile to the other person. One of the things that you should keep in mind is that effective communicators have mastery or at least a respectable amount of knowledge of what they are talking about. Hence, subject mastery should be part of your preparation.

How do you know if you have prepared enough for the meeting? It is quite hard to tell if the amount of preparation that you have is already enough or not, because a conversation can lead to so many things. But, ideally, you should be able to discuss the subject matter easily and smoothly. If you reach a point that talking and discussing the details of a particular topic is easy for you to do, then you are more likely to be ready to engage in an actual conversation. Of course, this means having a good amount of knowledge, and this knowledge can come from your preparation. Thanks to the Internet, you always have an access to a vast network of information. This will allow you to do your research in the comfort of your home. You may also want to read books and talk with and interview experts on the subject. This way you will be able to gain as much information that you need. Knowledge is important because if you do not know the subject matter of a conversation well, then it will be difficult for you to say something good and meaningful about it.

Another part of preparation is the physical preparation. It is a good practice to dress properly for the occasion. If you know that you are properly dressed and look decent enough, then you will be more confident to face and talk with other people. Needless to say, you need to be confident when you talk. If you are not confident, then people will find it difficult to trust you and believe whatever you say. You do not have to dress formally except, of course, if the situation requires it. However, you should always look presentable.

Unfortunately, you will not always be given time to make preparations. There are times when you will just find yourself in a conversation without any prior preparation. In this case, you can rely on other techniques as revealed in this book in order to keep the conversation effective and interesting. Of course, being able to prepare is a good advantage, so be sure to make use of it whenever possible.

#2 Listen

It is worth noting that effective communication is a two-way process. Unfortunately, many peoples think communication is just about being the one who is talking. This is wrong. From time to time, you should also be the one who is on the receiving end. One of the most important elements of effective communication is listening. To be more specific, this refers to *active listening.* It is unfortunate that although the importance of listening is a common advice, many people still fail to observe it. Keep in mind that listening means so much more than just hearing the other person's voice. When you listen, you should *understand* what the other person is saying. Another advice is to react to what the other person tells you. Giving a response ensures the other person that you are attentive to him and that you understand what he is saying.

There are certain differences between listening and active listening. Most people only know how to listen but they do not do it actively. So, how do you do active listening? When you actively listen to a person, you do not just hear his words. You should also ask questions and make appropriate responses to what the other person is telling you. Asking questions and reacting ensure the other person that he has your attention and that you are able to follow his train of thoughts. This is active listening. Listening, on the other hand, simply refers to hearing what the other person is telling you. Unfortunately, most people just know how to listen and do not make the other person feel that attention that you are actually giving him. When you actively listen to another, it will tend to make him feel loved and understood. Try talking to someone who actively listens to every word you say and you will know just how comforting it is to have someone to just talk to even if you do not get any solution to a problem. Indeed, many people are not really looking for a solution; they just want to have someone who would sincerely listen to them, someone who would hear whatever they say without judging them. Surprisingly, although this may seem an easy thing to do, most people are too preoccupied to even listen to another human being. Most of the time if they know that they would not gain anything from the conversation, they would rather avoid meeting the person. This book teaches its readers to value the existence and life of another person. Do not forget that the best time to talk with people effectively is not when you have something important to say, but when people actually want to talk with someone — and that someone could be you.

Do not commit the common mistake of being too self-centered. You should also take the time to hear and listen to what the other person has to say. If you are not willing to listen then it would be better for you to just talk with yourself. Remember: True effective communication is a two-way process. Before you even talk to somebody, be sure that you are also ready to listen. Unfortunately, many people become sort of narcissistic when they engage in conversation. They are too concerned with themselves that they fail to hear what the other person is telling them. Keep in mind that if you want to be a good communicator, then you should be a good listener.

Is it important for the other person to know that you are listening to him? The answer is *yes*. A common mistake committed by lots of people is to listen to a person without making him feel that they can hear him out. Take note that the person would not know that you can understand him unless you make positive responses. If the other person feels that you are actively listening to him, then you will more easily gain his trust, and he will feel more comfortable opening up to you. However, if the person feels that you are not giving him enough attention, then it would be hard to make him open up to you. Soon, he will feel very uncomfortable and even feel insulted if you do not make him feel that you are listening to him. So, how do you assure the other person that you are actively listening to him? Of course, you will not tell him, "Hey, I am listening to you." Rather, you will make him feel that you are actually listening to him while he is talking to you. You can easily do this by observing some simple practices like making eye contact and asking follow-up questions. For example, if a person says, "I am sad." ask him why he is sad. You cannot always expect people to open up to you immediately. Most of the time, you first need to make them feel that you want to listen to them and that you are someone whom they can trust. Once they feel how sincere you are and once they are comfortable enough talking with you, then that is the time when they will be more open to you. As you can see, the art of effective communication is not just about expressing your thoughts and ideas clearly, but is also about helping other people to express their thoughts and feelings and to share them with you.

Everyone will tell you that making eye contact is important. But, what if you find it uncomfortable to look at a person's eyes as you talk/listen? A good way to solve this problem is too look at the edge of his eye. This way, it will seem as if you are staring right at him. Another trick is to stare at the bridge of his nose right between his eyes. Of course the best way would still be to get used to looking at a person's eyes when you talk. Just practice it with every person you interact with, and you will soon get used to it. If you are truly sincere and would like to listen to another person, looking at his eyes would come naturally. As they say, "The eyes are the windows to the window."

From time to time, you may have to deal with people who are simply hard to listen to. Usually, these people are those who talk too much and simply have difficulty in expressing themselves clearly. Worse, they tend to talk loudly. So, how do you deal with these people? The principle remains the same: You have to listen. Now, if you find it hard to listen to everything that they are saying because you know that much of the things they are talking about do not really matter, the key is simply to identify keywords. You have to be patient with these people. You may find it irritating to listen to everything that they say, so a good tip is to just identify the real issue and ignore the others. Once you know the main issue, then you can always make an appropriate response. Sad to say, there are some people who have to talk for minutes just to say something that can be expressed in a few seconds. Again, effective communication teaches you to be good and respectable at all times.

You should also realize and appreciate that listening is an act of love and/or kindness. When you listen to another, you give him your time and attention. This is the kind of sincerity that people want. Needless to say, when somebody talks with you, you should stop whatever it is that you are doing and put your focus on the person who is talking. This is also the time to make eye contact with the person to assure him that you are listening to him.

A common mistake is to think that the person you are talking to is looking for a solution to a problem. The truth is that most people who talk about their problems are not really looking for a solution, but are merely looking for someone who would listen to them and understand them. Of course, the way to do this is by listening to the person who has a problem. These people simply want to be heard and understood. Unfortunately, many of these people feel that they are alone in the world, and so having someone who could listen and understand them would make them feel less alone. As you can see, the art of listening is a very important skill that you should master. In fact, expert communicators agree that listening is more important, if not as important, as talking. It is also by listening actively that you will be able to know how to best respond to a person. The more that you listen and understand a person, the easier it will be to connect with him on a deeper level.

#3 Ask the right questions

Learning to ask the right questions is a vital element of effective communication. It is also by asking questions that you can get to expound and deepen the level of conversation. It directs the flow of the conversation. By asking questions, you also assure the other person that you are actively listening to him and that you are able to follow his thoughts. However, do not be like other people who ask questions just for the sake of asking. Rather, every question that you ask must serve some purpose. A good advice is to ask only responsive questions. These are the questions that will get the story forward and develop the flow of conversation. For example, if a person says, "I took the bar exams." Ask him how he prepared for the exams and how he feels about them. This will definitely give you lots of information that you can use to further develop the level of conversation. By asking questions, you do not just make the person feel that you are listening to him, but it also encourages a person to talk more and open up to you. Needless to say, you should ask questions in a natural and gentle manner, and do not make the other person feel as if he were in some kind of investigation.

By asking questions, you make the other person feel that you are open to whatever it is that he has to say. Once again, effective communication is not just about you expressing your own thoughts and opinions. More importantly, it is about being open to other people and listening to whatever they have to say. Do not worry; you will also get your time to talk and share your own opinions.

Asking questions is also an excellent way to understand the other person. You should understand that effective communication is founded upon mutual respect and understanding. You need to understand each other. From time to time, you may have to tackle a sensitive topic where you may share different and even conflicting views. When you use effective communication, you can still talk about such matters without sacrificing peace and harmony between/among the parties. As the saying goes, "You can agree to disagree without sounding disagreeable." When you ask questions, you should also be ready to face answers that you may find unacceptable, but you need to learn to respect the other person. If you cannot respect a certain view or opinion, at least respect the other party as a person. After all, you are never obliged to adapt the same mindset or viewpoint. Indeed, from time to time, it is also important to appreciate the beauty in diversity.

Asking questions is one thing, asking the *right* questions is another. Expert communicators make sure to ask only the questions that will help develop a conversation. When you ask a question, that is the time when the other person will be expected to open up and share with you something, depending on your question. Be careful with the questions that you ask. Do not ask questions that would insult or offend the other person. If he feels that you are insulting him with your question then he will be more defensive, which will prevent you from having a meaningful conversation.

Most of the time, you only have to help the other person open up to you by asking him questions. For example, if a person says that he attended an event, ask him about the event. He will then tell you details about it. If you want to know more, then ask him more specific questions based on the information that he has also revealed to you. Simply stated, you only have to guide the person to share with you the whole story by asking him questions. This is the beauty of asking questions: You get to know more about the other person, and all that you need to do is ask.

#4 Share

Talking is sharing. Effective communication is about sharing and expressing yourself to people. Of course, you are expected to share something that the other person will like or at least find interesting.

But, what can you share? Every person has a story to tell. If not a story, then ideas, thoughts, opinions, and feelings that they can share with the world. Simply put, there is always something that you can share. The good thing about this is that you can share almost anything and everything that you want. However, effective communication is not just about sharing, but sharing something that the other person can also relate and connect to.

Do not underestimate the power of telling a good story. As they say, "Ideas come and go; stories stay." Sometimes it is most effective to tell whatever it is that you want to say in a narrative format. Stories usually have a way of expressing ideas more clearly. There is also power in stories that makes them hard to forget. Hence, you might want to use some storytelling when communicating effectively.

When you engage in a conversation, you should also expect for the other person to share something with you. You will have to take turns as to who will be the sender and the receiver, especially when telling a story. Do not worry; in every effective communication both or all parties will be given the chance the talk and share something. This is one of the things that set apart effective communication from just any other form of communication. Usually, when people think of the word *communication*, they only understand it to be a one-way process where you just have to talk whatever is on your mind. Worse, people usually do this carelessly without being careful of their choice of words. Hence, it is easy to understand why many people are not effective communicators.

When you share, you should also be open to feedbacks. After sharing something, you will most likely get a response from the receiver. Now, whatever response you get, remind yourself to remain calm and respectful. If you come to think of it, although it may seem that how a person responds is outside of your control, you actually have some control over it. This is because you can expect how a statement or story that you share would make the other person think or feel about it. For example, if you mention your recent success in life, then you can expect for your friend to be happy for you. Hence, before you share something, it is a good practice to pause for a moment and reflect how it would appear to the person with whom you want to tell it.

Effective communication aims to be able to build an environment and relationship based on trust where the parties are free to share everything with each other. This is one of the best things about learning effective communication. It also takes into account the relationship that you build with the other person. It is not just about expressing an idea, feeling, or thought. It also focuses on building good relationships.

When you share, especially when you share your weakness, it makes the other person feel that you can be trusted since you are the one who even reveal your vulnerability. People like honesty and openness. The only reason that usually prevents them for being open is because of some trust issue. But, if you take the initiative and be the one to remove your own walls and share, you can rest assured that it will be appreciated. Most of the time, it will make the other party feel that you are someone whom he can trust and rely on. Needless to say, you also have to be careful with what you share, especially if it is related to business or your profession.

Sharing can be a wonderful experience, especially if you know that the other person is sincere about it. When you share something, you give and entrust a part of you to another. In the same way, when a person shares something with you, you also receive something from him, perhaps an information, a secret, a story, or otherwise. The point is that when a person shares something, a connection is made. Now, it is only how you handle and respond to it which will determine if the connection is still worth having or not. Effective communicators know that value of sharing and respect whatever they receive from other people. Since they respect people regardless of their views, people also respect them. Never forget that effective communication is about building a good relationship. There is no reason to argue with one another. You only have to share and listen, and be respectful at all times.

The moment that you decide to talk to another, it is also a decision to finally be open to another human being. A common obstacle that prevents people from sharing or opening up to another is shyness. You need to understand that you should not allow shyness to prevent you from connecting with another person. Remember: As long as you are honest, then you do not have to be shy. If you focus on being shy, then you only make it stronger. If you continuously allow shyness to prevent you from having a good conversation, then you will not be able to experience the beauty of connecting with another person. Also, if you really feel uncontrollably shy, just remember that you are talking to just another human being. Feeling shy is normal. The best way to overcome shyness is by exposing yourself to more people. Soon, you will get used to it, and you will be more confident.

#5 Gestures

"Actions speak louder than words." Learn to use gestures effectively. Another thing that you should learn is how to read gestures. Also learn to understand facial expressions. Learning to use the right gestures is a good way to better illustrate your point, as well as to keep the conversation alive and interesting. Learning to read gestures will allow you to understand another person more clearly even before he says a word, or even when he says something that totally contradicts the truth. Gestures would reveal to you information that otherwise may be hidden from you. In fact, many people do not even realize how much information they share with others simply from their gestures. If you learn to understand the meaning behind the gestures, then you may be able to start reading people like a book. This means being more understanding of them.

It is also worth noting that not all gestures may signify a clear meaning. For example, some people associate a certain movement to mean that the person is lying. However, just because you see another person doing it does not mean that the said person is lying. This is where reading gestures can be tricky. However, it is still beneficial to know and understand the different gestures and their possible meanings. Although you cannot rely solely on gestures in understanding people, they can, nonetheless, still give you good insights not just about the subject matter of the conversation but also about the person with whom you are talking to.

One of the effective communicators who used gestures was Adolf Hitler. Yes, even Hitler knew the power of gestures that he studied his own gestures and learned to apply them more effectively. Feel free to learn the different gestures, as well as how you can apply them. There are helpful gestures that you can easily learn and use. These gestures can help you to illustrate a point more effectively and make the conversation more interesting. Of course, gestures alone are not enough. You should also communicate something that has meaning and value.

Learning to use gestures is a good way to be an effective communicator as it will also allow you to express your idea more clearly. It is also worth noting that gestures come naturally. However, there are those that have been used by humanity for ages that people associate them with a corresponding meaning. For example, closing your arms signify that you are taking a defensive position. However, some people simply like to cross their arms even for no reason. Hence, it is also good to know the meaning behind the gestures, so that you can correctly avoid using certain gestures that may cause misunderstanding and confusion, as well as to be able to get information from people even without talking directly to them. This will allow you to be able to understand people more effectively.

It can be stressing that gestures do not always mean what people say that they signify, hence, just because a person looks away after you ask him a question does not always mean that he is lying to you. Some people simply respond differently from the normal. A good way to know if your understanding of a certain gesture is correct or not is by testing it. After some time, you will get used to this to the point that you can tell if a specific gesture really intends to convey the meaning that has been associated with it or simply just a coincidence. This is something that comes with practice. One thing is sure: Learning about gestures can get you one step ahead of the conversation. If your job is something that requires convincing people and/or something that requires you to understand other people more completely, then learning to read gestures is something that should be in your arsenal. Although reading gestures is not always 100% accurate, it can, nonetheless, give you valuable insights which can be helpful.

Using gestures is also an excellent way to keep the conversation alive and interesting. Imagine talking to someone who does nothing but talk without using any gesture. Soon enough, you will surely get bored listening to him even if he is saying something interesting. Proper use of gestures can add action to the conversation, which will give it more life.

A common mistake is to use the same gesture over and over again. Most people who are not aware of effective communication simply allow themselves to use gestures unconsciously. Although gestures usually just happen even if you do not give it any thought, you will most likely be using the same gesture over and over again if you just allow it to express itself naturally. When this happens, your movement can look monotonous, and this may not look good to the person who is listening to you. Therefore, it is also a good advice for you to know the different gestures and then try to use them when you talk. A good way to practice with gestures is to watch yourself in the mirror as you talk. Pay attention to how you move and the gestures that you make. Also take note of your facial expressions, as well as how you project yourself. Make sure to use gestures naturally. Forcing to use a certain gesture may make you look awkward, so be sure to apply every gesture smoothly and in accordance with the thought or emotion that you are trying to convey.

#6 Trust

You need to remember that effective communication is based on trust. If the person you are talking with trusts you enough, then he will be more open to you. The more open and honest a conversation is, the more meaningful it will be. But, how do you make people trust you? You should understand that effective communication does not use deception. It is not about manipulating the other person. Rather, effective communication creates a bond of trust and confidence because you are worthy of being trusted. The key to this is sincerity. Unfortunately, some people think that they have to use tricks, deception, and lies to be an effective communicator. This is not true. In fact, although such lies may work to your advantage for some time, they will soon ruin your reputation in the long run. Hence, your focus should be on building a good relationship with people.

If you pay attention to the techniques in this book, as well as in other books, you will notice that the techniques are not really out of the ordinary, such as making eye contact, asking questions, and others. They are simply what a kind, decent, and sincere person would do if engaged in a conversation with someone whom he deeply cares about. Effective communication makes you to be that person. This is one of the reasons why learning to communicate effectively can change a person. The art of effective communication teaches one how to act as a gentleman or a kind and loving person.

It is usual for people to have walls as a form of defensive mechanism. After all, these days, it is hard to find people whom you can trust completely. However, these walls can be a barrier to an effective communication. You probably recognized these walls when you talk to someone who seems very reserved and does not open up to you. When this happens, the tendency is for you to be the one to do all the talking, which is not good. Although it is still considered communication, it is not *effective* communication. Again, communication is a two-way process. So, how do you make such kind of people to open up to you? An effective way is to show the person that it is okay to bring down his/her walls. To do this, you have to take the initiative and bring down your own walls to show the person that it is safe not to have any defenses. Show him your own vulnerability. In other words, trust the other person, and show him that you trust him. Most of the time, when you do this, the other person will appreciate your efforts and initiative and will start to lower his walls and begin to open up to you as well. When this happens, you can now engage in a more meaningful conversation.

When people study how to communicate with people more effectively, they often focus on themselves, specifically on how to express their thoughts and ideas more effectively. Although this is part of effective communication, the process does not end there. Unfortunately, they fail to realize that the person they are talking to are not effective communicators. Hence, instead of just focusing on yourself and what you have to say, you can have a more meaningful conversation by also helping the other person in expressing his thoughts, feelings, and ideas. When a person feels that it is easy and comfortable talking with you, then you will be able to gain his trust.

In our world today full of shrewd people who seek only for their own gain, it is not easy to find someone with whom you can talk about everything and feel good for doing so. This book teaches you how to be that person, and how you can turn a simple conversation into something that is meaningful and memorable.

Trust is important. If you have bad intentions, then this book is not for you. To make the other person trust you, then you should be worthy of being trusted. Usually, a good way to show the other person your own vulnerability is by showing him your own weaknesses. Normally, people will tend to be more open once they know that you are already being open to them. So, take the initiative and the risk and bring down your own walls first. Sometimes in order to be trusted, you need to be the first one to trust someone.

It is also important not to break a person's trust. Hence, be sure to always be true to your words and do not resort to any falsehood. Also, if a person has entrusted you with a secret, make sure to keep it a secret forever. Trust, once broken, is almost impossible to restore. Take very good care of it.

#7 Be more connected

This is the part where you deepen the level of conversation and get more connected. Normally, this part happens on its own and is simply about observing the aforesaid techniques continuously. This is mainly about building a stronger relationship. Talking to a person does not usually happen just once. If you get to feel comfortable with each other, then you will most likely meet up again and talk some more. In fact, if you come to think of it, the relationships in the world share the very same activity: talking. It is by talking with one another that people negotiate things. It is also how people share thoughts and ideas on a regular basis. Hence, if you want to be more connected, then it would mean having more conversations with the same person or persons. This is simply how the world works: People get connected by talking with one another.

When you talk with people, a suggested approach is to consider every person that you talk to as special. It does not matter whether you are talking with your boss at work, a colleague, friend, spouse, or any one at all. The key is to see everyone as special and to treat them in a special way. Sadly, people have already forgotten just how meaningful talking should be. This is exactly why learning how to talk effectively is important, especially in today's world where people easily take things for granted.

It is important for you to realize what it really means to *talk*. If done with sincerity and kindness, talking creates a connection that can go beyond the physical. Have you experienced having a soulful connection with someone? This can be achieved through effective communication. Once people trust each other and become more open, other positive energies like love, kindness, hope, and even happiness, can be channeled through talking — and this can create a truly meaningful and powerful bond.

Repeated meetings and talks can make a bond or relationship much stronger. Of course, you are expected to continuously apply the techniques as revealed in this book. As you can see by now, these techniques are not something that you apply today and forget tomorrow. Rather, they become *you*. Perhaps this is one of the reasons why some people find it hard to communicate effectively: They are not sincere enough to do it. To talk effectively, you cannot just fake being sincere or listening to people. You should be truly sincere and actually listen to whatever they tell you. This is something that you cannot just act out intentionally. If you are not sincere enough, then the other person will most likely feel your insincerity. How can you look at a person in the eyes and say that you care if you do not feel like caring at all? Hence, if you want to turn yourself into an effective communicator, you should also improve yourself as a person. Self-improvement is part of the process.

The more connected you are to a person, the more the communication will deepen. This is another reason why you should not fake being sincere; it is because it would not last long. If you are not true enough, then the other person will soon recognize it. You should also realize that even if you talk effectively, it does not guarantee that anyone would love to talk with you. After all, talking effectively does not mean pleasing or entertaining everyone whom you talk with. Hence, do not expect for people to flock around you and like you for being an effective communicator. Rather, just know that by learning these techniques, you will be able to connect more intimately with people, and that this art of talking would make you a better human being.

Chapter 3: Best Practices

Learn from the experts

When learning to communicate effectively, you will most likely try to learn from experts who claim to have mastered the art of effective communication. Feel free to visit their blogs and read their books on the subject. However, just be careful, because not everyone who claims to be an expert in effective communication is a real expert. In today's world, it is fairly easy to promote one's self as an expert in anything. Therefore, take whatever you read or hear with a grain of salt. The best way to know if a certain technique actually works is by testing it.

Although it is good to learn from experts, it is strongly suggested that you do not depend on them completely. Do not forget that effective communication is an art. Therefore, you should also develop your own style of conversing with people.

It is also a good idea to closely study how the real experts communicate. For example, play a certain video and pay attention to how an expert talks, his gestures, how he uses pauses, tone of voice, and others.

A good way to learn from experts is by watching their videos. You might want to try YouTube for this. Pay attention to how these "experts" talk and get a message across very clearly. It is also advised that you videos of famous orators and observe how they deliver their message powerfully. Take note of their choice of words, voice, posture and gestures, as well as the way that they project themselves to the audience. Orators are usually great communicators who are able to deliver a message powerfully. Of course, their techniques may not always be applicable to a day-to-day conversation, but you can still learn from them, especially from the way they use words to express their thoughts and emotions.

Find your voice

You need to find your voice as early as possible. Usually, a beginner will try to imitate how an expert talks. This is not a good approach. The thing is that no matter how hard you try, you cannot completely duplicate another person's style of talking with people. Instead, what you should do is to develop your own style by using your own voice.

Finding your own voice takes trial and error. Many times it is knowing what your voice *is not* that will lead you to find the voice that is truly your own. Every person has his or her own voice. Take note that this does not refer to your literal *voice*, but is rather something about the way you connect with other people. It is also something that you develop as you continue to practice effective communication.

Effective communication is an art. There are many ways to apply the same techniques. To help you find your voice, you can try to adapt different styles of communicating and see which one best suits your personality. The best way to know your unique voice is to just be yourself. Do not think about being successful or being an effective communicator. Simply be yourself and talk naturally. Of course, this does not mean that you should be careless in your approach. However, it should be noted that aside from applying the techniques, it is also important to be yourself when you talk.

Talk clearly

When you talk, make sure that you pronounce all the words clearly. Some people tend to "eat" their words or talk too fast. Help the receiver to understand your message by conveying it in a clear and easy-to-understand manner. A good advice to be able to talk more clearly is to talk slowly and make sure that you pronounce all the words clearly and correctly. Also, be as concise as possible. Avoid using statements that are too wordy. Avoid unnecessary words and go straight to the point.

If you have problems with stammering, then a good way to avoid or at least lessen such problem is by talking more slowly. Now, it takes practice to do this, especially if you are used to talking too fast. However, this is something that you can easily learn with continuous practice. The key is to always remind yourself to talk clearly. A common mistake is only to practice it when you need it. What you should do is to make it a part of your day-to-day conversations. Keep in mind that how you talk in your day-to-day conversations will most likely be the way you talk when you attend meetings, events, and others. Also, effective communication embraces all forms of conversations, so it is only right that you apply the techniques every time you engage in any conversation, including the usual day-to-day talks that you engage in.

You should also learn how to regulate your voice. Learn when to use a high tone and a low tone, also learn when to whisper. If you observe expert communicators, you will notice how they play with their voice and use it strategically. They project their voice powerfully and deliver the message that they want to get across very clearly. Also, being too monotonous can be boring, so regulate your voice and avoid following a single rhythm.

Be flexible

Effective communication requires one to be flexible enough. Hence, it does not have any fixed rule to follow. How you approach a subject will most likely depend on the circumstances of a situation. It is also worth noting that you cannot always expect to talk with someone who shares the same view as you have. Hence, you should also be flexible enough to welcome other points of view.

Depending on the person with whom you are talking to, you may also have to adjust how you talk from time to time. This is not about being untrue to yourself, but merely for the sake of being more effective. After all, you cannot expect for everyone to respond in the same way. If a certain technique does not work on a certain person, then you might want to try another technique in its place.

Being flexible also refers to the ability of controlling yourself. Sometimes you may have to control your reaction and choice of words. Do not forget that part of effective communication is learning how to make the other person feel more respected and comfortable. Of course, being flexible does not mean that you should aim to please the other person. It bears stressing that you are not obliged in any way to please the other person. There is a difference between pleasing another person and allowing him to be more comfortable with you.

Not everyone will respond to you the way that you expect or would want them to. You will also definitely meet people who are very hard to predict, and some would even be rude to you. You should be flexible enough to handle all these types of people. This may be hard for beginners, but if you practice enough, then you will soon be able to handle any kind of conversation and people. Talking to people is an art. There is no rule as to how you should respond or react, and there is also no rule as to what you should tell the other person. You are always free to express yourself. Unfortunately, many people are not good at expressing themselves. You should be flexible enough to deal with such kind of people. You may have to be more patient and make some adjustments just to talk with them effectively. Sometimes the art of talking is like a dance where you also need to make some adjustments in order to move harmoniously with another. There is strict rule that will work for all occasions. This is why you need to find your own voice and set your rhythm.

Be respectful

Be respectful at all times. No matter what happens, never allow your temper or emotion to control the conversation. You should always stay calm and relaxed. A good characteristic of any effective communicator is the respect with which he carries himself. By being respectful, the other person will also feel that he should respect you. Now, it is easy to show respect if you are talking to someone who is very kind and nice. But, what if you find yourself dealing with a difficult person, or a person who only wants to get into a debate with you? In such instances, you may find your temper and patience being put the test. During such time, you should remain respectful. Never succumb to anger. As the saying goes, "Always be a gentleman. Not because the other person is a gentleman, but because you are."

Respect is very important to any relationship, even in a conversation of any kind. No matter how the other person treats you, be sure to treat him kindly. Sometimes it is by respecting other people that they will learn how to respect you. Respect can earn respect.

Have an open mind

It is important for you to keep an open mind when you engage in a conversation. When you converse with a person, you may encounter strange and even contradicting ideas. You get to brainstorm ideas with each other. If you do not have an open mind, then some of the ideas may seem very wrong and revolting. But, if you keep an open mind, then you can have a healthy conversation with anyone. Take note that you do not need to convince the other person to adapt your way of thinking. In the same way, you are not expected to agree with everything that the other person is saying. You are always free to disagree. Just remember to express your disagreement politely and respectfully. You need to understand that you disagree with a certain view or opinion but not necessarily with the person. Hence, you can always have respect for a person despite his contradicting and even erroneous views. Good communicators know that a person is not always what he says when he talks. In fact, many people are not good at expressing themselves. Therefore, it is very important for you to keep an open mind at all times. By having an open mind, you will also be more open to new and interesting ideas. People also like talking to someone who has an open mind. They want to open up to people whom they know will not judge them no matter what they say. This is another important lesson to remember: Having an open mind means not judging a person no matter what he tells you. Instead, what you should do is to try to understand more the other person. You are not there to judge, but to listen. If you cannot listen and sympathize with another, then perhaps it would be better if you do not engage in a conversation. Again, effective communication is not just about you. It is two-way process. Just as there is a time for you to talk, there is also a time for you to listen.

Have a sense of humor

Learn to laugh — laugh even at yourself and your mistakes. If you notice expert communicators, they usually add some humor to their talks. A humor can release some tension and make people feel more comfortable. Therefore, it is a good practice to use some humor from time to time. However, just be sure to use a humor whenever it is proper. Using humor can make a serious conversation to seem lighter. However, keep in mind that there are also times when the setting is completely serious without any place to drop some humor. Make sure to observe proper timing; otherwise, a humor might be taken out of context and be received as an insult.

Adding some humor is not always an easy thing to do. There is also no assurance that the other person will like it. Hence, if you notice that the person whom you are talking to is trying his best to humor you, show your appreciation for his efforts. Of course, you should also do the same favor and try to use a little humor in your conversation. Also, engaging in a very serious conversation for hours can be very boring and can even make you feel exhausted easily. A good humor, especially when followed by a good laugh, can make you feel less stressed and more comfortable. Therefore, whenever possible, try to use some humor in your conversations.

Learn to use pauses

A pause can be a powerful tool in effective communication. A pause can draw more attention, arouse interest, or it can also give emphasis to something. One of the effective communicators who used a pause properly was Adolf Hitler. Hitler used to pause for few seconds before starting his speech. A pause draws attention, and you will be sure that you have all the attention and focus of the audience the moment you start talking. A pause can also be used to build up the suspense and make the conversation more interesting.

You should remember to use pauses wisely and sparingly. Using too many pauses may not be a good idea; therefore, only use it when you have a clear purpose for doing so. If it does not serve a good purpose, then do not apply it.

Focus on the relationship

You need to realize that talking to people is about building a good relationship. It means so much more than just getting a message across or listening to what the other person has to say. Focus on relationship-building. The more that you are able to build a good relationship, the better the conversation will be.

A common mistake is focusing more on the gain that you expect to get from the conversation. This is true, especially when you attend business meetings. Of course, you will not sacrifice the interest of your business. But, you also need to be cautious of projecting an image of being too greedy. People will find it hard to trust you if they notice that you only care about your own interest.

An effective way to build a good relationship is to focus on the interest of the other person. If you talk about something that the other person is interested in, then you will definitely capture his interest, and he will most likely enjoy talking with you. It is not a surprise that business meetings usually end up with talks about golf, cars, and others. When this happens, friendship starts to develop, and a more meaningful relationship takes shape. Also, when you do this, people will usually appreciate it and tend to be more open and friendly.

Continuous practice

Truly learning effective communication takes more than just reading books and theories about it. In order to become an effective communicator, you need to take positive actions and engage in continuous practice. As already stated, you should apply the techniques of effective communication even in your day-to-day conversations. Remember that every conversation you have is another opportunity to apply and improve your communication skills. After some time, all the techniques and habits of effective communication will be a part of who you are as a person. By then, you will realize that communicating effectively is not a difficult task. By improving your character, you also improve your level of communication. In a way, it can be said that learning how to communicate effectively is about learning to become a better person. This is one of the reasons why learning to become a better and effective communicator is highly beneficial. It also improves you as a person. Not to mention, those who can communicate effectively are usually those who get rewarded since they are the ones who excel at what they do.

You cannot just turn into an expert communicator overnight. Even if you read all the books about talking to people, you still need to spend time and efforts to actually learn the techniques. Of course, the only way to learn them is by active and continuous application.

For starters, it is advised that you focus on learning the techniques one at a time. Hence, you might want to focus on active listening before moving on to other techniques and tips. As you improve and get used to the process of effective communication, you can then apply two or more techniques at the same time. Of course, once you get good at this, you should soon be able to use all the techniques at once and handle any kind of conversation effectively and confidently. Speaking about confidence, it is also an important ingredient of effective communication. The more that you practice, the more confident you will be. Unfortunately, many people who try to learn how to talk effectively do not practice enough. Keep this in mind: Actual practice is very important. You need to try to apply the techniques regularly. Also, do not just wait for people to come and talk to you. You should take the initiative and be more social and talk to people. For purpose of practicing the techniques, it is strongly suggested that you make sure to talk to at least one person everyday and be sure to apply the techniques in this book. Do not be discouraged if you are not able to execute them properly. Practice makes perfect, so spend more time practicing the teachings in this book. Soon, you will get used to it and these techniques will be second nature to you that you would not even have to think about them. Instead, they will be a habit that becomes a natural part of who you are. If you watch the videos of expert communicators, you will notice that they are always very relaxed. This is because they do not even think about the techniques. This is because once you reach that level, these techniques are no longer considered techniques but are already a part of who you are as a person. Again, it bears stressing that learning to talk effectively can be a life-changing journey that is full of positive changes.

Conclusion

Thanks for making it through to the end of this book. I hope it was informative and able to provide you with all of the tools you need to achieve your goals whatever they may be.

The next step is to apply everything that you have learned. Learning to talk to people effectively requires continuous practice. It is worth remembering that talking to people is something that is innate in human beings. Hence, do not see the techniques in this book as something difficult to do. Take note that you already have all these skills; you simply have to develop them. If you are just starting out, you may expect to have some difficulty in applying the techniques and tips in this book. This is normal, so do not be discouraged. Just persist in your practice, and you will soon notice some improvements. Learning to communicate more effectively is just like learning any other new skill. Even if you have all the instructions that you may need, it will still take and practice before you can completely learn how to use the techniques properly.

As you may have already noticed by now, there is really no secret to effective communication. It is only about being and acting more human and knowing that you are connecting with another human being. It is by realizing this truth that makes the activity of talking meaningful and valuable. When you talk, you open yourself up to people. Depending on the quality of the words that you say, you either send positive or negative energy out into the world. In the same manner, when you are the receiver and listens to another, you receive whatever the other person is opening up to you. The process of communication is a beautiful exchange that takes place between two or more human beings.

It is worth noting that you should not limit yourself to the techniques in this book, as well as other books on the same subject. Talking effectively to people is an art; therefore, do not let any teaching to put limitation as to how talking should be. Feel free to modify the techniques and even come up with your own set of techniques. Since talking can be considered an art, use it in a way that you express yourself more beautifully and effectively.

As you learn and apply the techniques of effective communication, you will notice some positive changes in your life. Most likely, you will notice how people respond more favorably when you talk to them effectively. You may even make new friends and show excellence in what you do. More importantly, learning how to talk effectively will make you more human and make you conscious of the beauty that comes with connecting to another human being. Unfortunately, since people talk and talk every day, many tend to take things for granted that they fail to see how wonderful it is to connect and talk with another human being. Learning to talk effectively to people will remind you of what truly matters and make you a better human being.

There is joy in being able to talk effectively to people. Indeed, this is a "skill" that is worth learning. By now, you should already have a good foundation and understanding of how to talk to people effectively. Feel free to review the techniques and even come up with your own. More importantly, be sure to apply your knowledge. Effective communication requires continuous practice. Stop being shy or worrying; it is time for you to enjoy connecting with another soul: Talk and connect with another human being.

HOW TO
INFLUENCE PEOPLE
THE RIGHT WAY
The Only 7 Steps You Need to Master Persuasion,
Manipulation and Impacting People Today
DEAN MACK

BOOK 2: HOW TO INFLUENCE PEOPLE

THE RIGHT WAY

The Only 7 Steps You Need to Master Persuasion, Manipulation and Impacting People Today

Dean Mack

Respective authors own all copyrights not held by the publisher.

The information herein is offered for informational purposes solely, and is universal as so. The presentation of the information is without contract or any type of guarantee assurance.

The trademarks that are used are without any consent, and the publication of the trademark is without permission or backing by the trademark owner. All trademarks and brands within this book are for clarifying purposes only and are the owned by the owners themselves, not affiliated with this document.

Table of Contents

Introduction... 66

Chapter 1: Have Confident Body Language 67

Chapter 2: Make People Like You 74

Chapter 3: Be Clear and Concise.............................. 80

Chapter 4: Ask for Favors.................................... 86

Chapter 5: Make Emotional Connections.......................... 92

Chapter 6: Be More Transparent 98

Chapter 7: Take an Interest in Others........................104

Chapter 8: Summary of Steps 109

Conclusion 113

Introduction

Congratulations on purchasing this book and thank you for doing so.

The following chapters will discuss the 7 most important steps for influencing the people around you. You will learn the best tricks and techniques to master persuasion and manipulation so that others listen to you all of the time.

Getting others to do what you want is not impossible, and you can certainly train yourself to have influence over others. Even if this is not a natural skill that you have, the information provided in this book can teach it to anyone willing to learn.

Many people want to gain control over others only because they want to feel dominant above everyone else. Some people though wants to be influential not because they want to, but because they need to. If you are an employer, a supervisor, or a team manager, or just someone who struggles influencing – or taking control – of others, then this is the perfect book for you.

There are plenty of books on this subject on the market, thanks again for choosing this one! Every effort was made to ensure it is full of as much useful information as possible. Please enjoy!

Chapter 1: Have Confident Body Language

If you want to learn how to influence others, you will first need to know how to portray confident body language. Body language communicates more with others than our words do, and it can make the difference when trying to get others to listen to us. This form of non-verbal communication refers to any expression or gesture that we make to deliver a message to another person.

Oftentimes our body language can make an impression on someone before we get the chance to do so verbally. Imagine walking up to someone that was slumped over with a frown on their face. Your first impression of this person would be that they are upset and sad. Without even talking to the person, you have already drawn your own conclusions about them. This is true for how others view you as well, which is why you want to convey a positive, confident image.

By expanding your body and portraying a confident image, you will alter the way that others view you. Along with this, you will also begin to view yourself in a more positive light and will feel even more powerful in your endeavors to influence other people.

While body language is essential for first impressions, it is also important to maintain confident body language as you carry on a conversation. This is because your body language will help to supplement your spoken message or make it come across more believably. You will need a strong delivery when telling others what you want them to do. Otherwise, they will not take you seriously.

As you come to understand the importance of having proper body language, you must then learn how you can do it yourself. There are many aspects of body language that will matter when trying to influence others, which we will cover.

Your body language should not make it seem as though you are anxious or nervous in any way. You also do not want to make it seem like you are uptight or too serious. To find balance, you should watch yourself in the mirror and critique your own body language. As you go through each aspect of body language to improve upon, you can practice in a mirror until you feel ready to use it around someone else. You will need to make sure that you seem natural, but also somewhat intimidating so that others still take you seriously.

To begin identifying areas that you should improve on in terms of body language, start by looking at your posture. Posture will be the key to how you carry yourself for when others begin to form an opinion of you. To work in this area, start by pressing your chest slightly outward and moving your stomach in. Keep your shoulders held back and keep your head up. Be sure to check yourself in a mirror to make sure that you are not overextending any part of your body so that you still look as natural as possible. Practice holding this position frequently until it becomes natural. Over time, you will find that your body will naturally sit this way without you having to think about it or look in a mirror.

Keeping your head up high is essential for good posture, but is also going to be a large determining factor on how others perceive you. If you are keeping your head down, you are indicating that you are not the one in control of the conversation or situation. By keeping your head up, you make it possible to take control of a situation so that you can start to influence those around you and convey confidence in your abilities to do so.

Once your posture is sufficient, you may then begin to work on your eye contact. Sometimes maintaining eye contact with others can feel awkward or intimidating, but you can get past these feelings to influence others. You should focus on keeping eye contact with other people in every conversation you have. This will make people respect you more and will let them know that you are still listening to what they have to say. If someone does not think you are listening to them, they will be less likely to care about what you are saying in return and will be harder to influence.

You should also take care to not offer too much eye contact, as this can be too aggressive and may seem strange to the other person. If the other person feels threatened by you, they are not any more likely to listen to you than if you had not maintained any eye contact at all. Again, you will need to practice this skill and become more conscious of it in each conversation that you have.

Now that you have learned how to master proper posture and eye contact, you will also need to learn how to form sufficient gestures. The most common ones that you will utilize are smiling and handshakes, so learning these first is essential.

The most important thing to note for smiling to influence others is that you must time it appropriately. Smiling can be your most powerful method of influence or your most dangerous one, depending on how you go about it. You do not typically want to walk into a crowded room with a smile on your face immediately. You first want people to recognize your attendance and build a presence in the room. Once there has been an opportunity for this, you can smile as you wish. Be sure to smile when it is fitting, such as for excitement or in a positive interaction. You also want to be sure that your smiles are natural and legitimate, as it is often easy to see through a fake smile. By mastering this, others will feel connected to you and will be more likely to be influenced by you later on.

As for handshakes, you will need to convey a sense of power. A firm and strong handshake will immediately grab the attention of others when you greet them, as it shows that you respect them, as well as yourself. You may also want to be the first one to initiate the handshake, as this conveys a sense of authority to the other person that may be difficult to obtain otherwise. For example, if you are about to interview for a position, you may benefit from extending your hand first so that you are one step ahead of the interviewer, which they are likely to respect whether they are cognizant of it or not. Once you have started the handshake, allow it to last for up to about 5 seconds before pulling away.

Fidgeting may also be an issue that you struggle with when it comes to confident body language. People who are nervous tend to move their hands or their bodies without purpose, which is easily noticed and does not give off a professional vibe. You may need to consciously find a place to put your hands or a position that you do not move back and forth in to halt any nervous movements you might be doing. Take careful note of when these movements are happening so that you may pinpoint why and what you can do to stop them. For example, if you are someone that plays with their hair when nervous, you may find that tying your hair back stops you from doing this. You may also be doing this because it puts you at ease, but others can recognize it as nerves that are making you do it.

You will also need to make sure that your body language shows that you are engaged. This will be accomplished somewhat with smiling and eye contact, but there are extra steps you should take as well. To do this, you want to make sure that you are reacting while listening to a conversation. As mentioned, the other person must recognize that you are listening to them before they will be willing to listen to you. You can accomplish this by nodding throughout the conversation, as well as mirroring any movements or expressions made by the other person. The movements that they are making reflect how they feel, and by doing a similar movement, you will show them that you feel a similar way and that you recognize their feelings.

Purposefully utilizing your arms and legs will also be important for body language. Even if you are not using your arms or legs to communicate, their placement will be essential to the vibe that you are giving off. For example, if your arms are crossed over your chest during a conversation, you are suggesting that you feel uncomfortable or that you do not like talking to the other person. To avoid this, you can first become more aware of where your arms and legs are. By recognizing their placement, you can learn to adjust accordingly. You can place your arms on your side or keep your legs crossed to look relaxed and engaged. However, you will need to remember to keep your placements natural as well. Otherwise, it will negate your efforts to show that you are involved and interested in the conversation.

After reviewing all of the previous information on body language, you should also take time to note the culture you are in and what is considered to be acceptable. Every culture has their own forms of body language that are considered professional or friendly, so you will need to be careful to not come off the wrong way. There are also some forms of body language that are disrespectful, which will also be important to learn about. If you are interacting in a setting that may have a different style of body language from what you are used to, you will need to acclimate yourself to the rules of that culture so that you are still able to influence others effectively. For example, in the United States, maintaining proper eye contact is important, as we already covered. However, you would not want to utilize the same eye contact principles in Japanese culture. This is because Japanese people tend to only make eye contact at the beginning of a conversation and find it awkward to maintain it from there. You would not be as likely to have influence over another person in this culture if you tried to make the same amount of eye contact as you do in the United States.

Body language is an essential skill that you must learn if you want to have influence and power over other people. This form of communication is crucial in making an impact on others so that they will listen to you and respect you. Once you have mastered this skill, you will be ready to move forward in the process of influencing people effectively.

Chapter 2: Make People Like You

When you meet someone for the first time, you may find it hard to remember what they looked like or what they said. However, you are far more likely to remember how that person made you feel. Whether they made you feel nervous or happy, your memories and impressions of the person are based on how you felt when talking to them.

The next step in learning to influence others is to make people like you. You will need to learn how to make good impressions so that you are memorable and respected enough to be listened to.

One of the main factors in how likable you are is your charisma. This charm to your personality is what will attract others so that they are drawn in and open to listening to what you have to say. Most of us have some room for improvement in this area, which is why it should be the first consideration when trying to make others like you.

To become more charismatic, you should first attempt to make yourself more present. As we covered in the last chapter, engagement during a conversation is incredibly important. This is true even now, as getting rid of any distractions will be appreciated by the other person that you are talking to. When your full

attention is in the conversation, it becomes yours to control.
Because people desire attention, providing this when
communicating gives you the upper hand so that you may begin to
influence in whatever way you choose.

Another way to be charismatic is to be sure that you are not
focusing on your response while someone else is talking. This goes
along with making sure your full attention is in the conversation,
but can still be easy to forget. The tendency to think about own
responses is hard to ignore, but it distracts from what is being said
and shows that you are not listening as much as you should be. It
is alright to think about your response when the other person has
stopped talking, and will even give you a better opportunity to
collect your thoughts and consider everything they said so that
your response is appropriate. This will also be much more
appreciated and will enhance the communication for you to
influence.

The main goal of being more charismatic is to make people feel
good. When you have this power over people, the rest of the
influencing you do becomes much easier. However, there are still
many other ways to make people like you to influence them as
well.

One of the ways to make people like you more is to demonstrate
power over them. Most people respond well to authority figures,
although this may not work for everyone you encounter. However,

you may notice that people give into you much more easily and do as you say.

To convey a sense of power, you should first double check your body language. As we covered in the previous chapter, this will be your first impression on others and can give you a head start on gaining power and making people like you. Once this has been accomplished, you can start finding other ways to gain power over others.

One simple way to demonstrate power in a situation is to take control of the environment. This can be moving the objects around you or being the first one to initiate a conversation. While you do not want to be fidgeting too much when doing this, it is ok to pick up an item or two just to show that you can. You may also try initiating a handshake to establish power in your situation. You can be creative with this task and adjust it as needed to your environment.

People will also like you more when you are humble. While you do not want to sell yourself short, it is important to respect the knowledge that others can give to you. Even if you are influential, you will still need to learn from other people and acknowledge what they can offer you.

Practicing humility will also include praising others. People like to know that they are doing a good job and that you think highly of the work that they do. By demonstrating this, others will like and respect you more. You will need to give people the credit that they deserve for what they do if you ever want to have any influence over them. Imagine having a boss that took all of the credit for the work that you did and never praised you for doing any of it. While the boss might still have actual power over your job, they would likely have little influence over what you did otherwise because you do not get the credit that you deserve for your work. Anyone would feel underappreciated and resentful in a situation like this one.

Another piece of advice for being humble is to take a step back. This means allowing others to speak more and allowing them to do something first. You may be eager to talk or do everything you can when trying to gain influence, but this can often hinder your ability to do so. It also helps to give others the perception that they are the ones in control of a situation, which being humble will help with. If performed correctly, the other person will do most of the talking and will go first in any tasks that need to be completed. This will give you the chance to listen to them and pay attention to what matters. They will also like that they feel in control and will also feel more connected with you.

Do not be afraid to admit your mistakes. This is another part of practicing humility because you must recognize when you are wrong and have messed up. It is hard for people to like being around someone who thinks that they are always right and do not know when to admit that they are wrong. If you are conscious of this and attempt to do it yourself as often as possible, you will notice that others are appreciative of it.

Another way to get people to like you more is to be positive. Your mood and emotions have a powerful influence on others that they likely do not even notice. When you are happy and positive, those around you will start to become this way as well. You will also notice that people are attracted to you more when you are positive, and they will also be more willing to listen to you. Do not be afraid of displaying happiness around other people, even if their mood is somewhat down. They will soon begin to reflect your good mood subconsciously, which will give you the upper hand to be the one with power in the situation.

Being more positive might also involve making other people laugh. There is a time and place for joking around, but sometimes it is a good way to get people to like you. It can lighten the mood and make others feel more comfortable around you. Be sure to tell jokes that are appropriate for the situation. No one wants to hear a sexual joke during a serious conversation, and it is a quick way to ruin your credibility. Timing will be everything with this suggestion, so be sure to use it wisely.

You will also find that sharing common traits with others makes them like you more as well. These traits can be good or bad, as either way will form a connection. Humans are attracted to people that are similar to them, so identifying characteristics, traits, and qualities that you have in common with someone else will instantly make them like you more. This is one of the most important ways to make people like you more and can be used on just about any person you meet. No matter who they are, you will have at least one or two things in common with them that you can bond over. By making this connection, you will be more likable and will gain influence as needed.

When people like you they are more likely to listen to you. This may seem obvious, but it is not always be easy for everyone to accomplish. Some have the natural talent of walking into a room and making everyone they meet enjoy their company. Even if this isn't you, it is possible to make it happen.

All of the previous bits of information will help you get people to enjoy being around you in just about any situation. You will need to make people feel good and validated in your communications with them and show that you are humble and respect them as well. The more interested that you are in other people, the more interested they will be in you.

Once you have learned and practiced all of the suggestions outlined in this chapter, you will be ready to move on to become more concise and clear to gain influence over others.

Chapter 3: Be Clear and Concise

Persuading others can be a daunting task, and it is easy to be a bit nervous when trying to do so. However, there are a few ways that you can prepare yourself so that your persuasive skills work. The most important way being that your words need to be both clear and concise, as the chapter title indicates. This may take some work, but once mastered it will be one of the most effective ways to influence other people.

This chapter might take you back to the writing classes you took in school, as the learning principles are similar. It can often be difficult to translate what we want to say into actual words, such as with writing or speaking. By exploring ways of going about this, you can become a much better talker so that others do what you say.

To start becoming clearer when you speak, you will need to not be so "wordy." This means to simplify most of the verbs that you use, or any sentences in general. You may tend to use abstract phrases or terms when you want to sound smart, but this is unnecessary. If anything, doing this makes it obvious to the other person that you are trying to impress and influence them. You also run the possibility of misusing words or stumbling over phrases, thus losing your credibility even if you had previously been successful.

To practice simplifying what you say, pay attention to the verbs that you are using. For example, instead of saying "Her movements are suggestive of..." you could say "Her movements suggest..." in place of the other verbiage. A change like this may seem insignificant, but it makes more message clear without any extra "fluff" added on to it. The example given is also just a small bit of a phrase, as you will have more than just a word or two to alter.

Simplifying your message should also include using more active verbs instead of passive. Examples of passive words include "we have" and "there are." Instead, you should declare what you want as you speak. An example of an active sentence would be, "I believe that we must place the dresser on the right side of the bed." The previous example conveys what you want and not that it "should" or "could" be done. You do not have to sound demanding with this kind of verbiage, but you demonstrate your own decisiveness and give a simple command of what you want.

Another way you can simplify your words is to work on using fewer vague phrases and nouns. By using vague words, you draw yourself into saying even more to make up for it so that your message still makes sense. Some examples of vague words include area, place, situation, aspect, degree, and consideration. An example of a vague phrase you might use would be, "Let's go to that place across the street with good tacos." Instead of saying the previous sentence, you could say, "Let's go to the taco restaurant across the street." You may be using vague words without realizing it, so you may need to analyze how you speak frequently. It is hard to change how you speak when you have been doing it for a long time, but it will pay off. What you say will be clear and to the point, minus all of the unnecessary verbiage you were using previously.

Once you have cleaned up what you say, you can start to make your words more concise. This step is equally as important as clarity, as the two together will make you much more respectable and persuasive. The overall goal is for you to make your messages quick and understandable so that people listen and remember what you say. Being concise means that you are going to use a few words to say a lot. This also means that you will need to choose your words wisely.

To be concise, the most important step you can take is to think before you say anything. This will allow your words to feel more natural, but also considerate and necessary. This will allow you the opportunity to compose your thoughts and sort them down into a simple message. You do not want to take more than 5 seconds to do this, as this would often make the situation awkward. However, these few seconds are all you need to stop yourself from blurting out the first words that come to your mind. Instead, you will be able to say what you mean without filler.

The next way to make what you say more concise is to start and end with your main idea. Humans tend to remember the beginning and the end of what we are taught. For example, in a lecture, you might remember what was said initially and right before you left, but a lot of what was said in between might be hard to remember. Given this, it is important to remember when speaking so that you can plan your words accordingly. You should start and end with the most important concepts so that people remember what matters. This will also help to guide your listeners and make them think about what you are saying. By introducing them early to what you want, it becomes more memorable, and they are more likely to do it.

Once you have mastered getting your most important concepts and desires out first and reiterating them at the end, you need to learn what to say in between so that people still listen to you. The middle of your message should still consist of important information, but only that which supports the main idea. This should include only the most important details and nothing that could be written off as irrelevant. You need to allow yourself to give the most effective communication possible to get people to listen to you and remember what you say.

Paying attention to your filler sounds while talking is important as well. You need to 'clean up' your sentences and avoid the 'ums' and 'ohs' that tend to happen that hinder the effectiveness of what you are saying. You should practice speaking on your own time to observe how often you make these noises while talking so that you can work on stopping them. These noises also delay you from getting to the point of your message, which is distracting for your audience. A lot of this is avoided by taking time to think about what you are going to say, but may still be difficult to avoid without practice.

While having a clear, concise message is vital to getting people to do what you want, you must also be sure to tailor your message to your audience. The suggestions outlined in this chapter would likely not be the way you would talk to a friend in a casual setting, but it would be if you were trying to get them to do something for you. You should identify who you are talking to and what it is that they need to know. Knowing your audience will help you to avoid awkward communication and will allow you to figure out how much you should say.

As previously stated, knowing your audience will help you to determine what they need to know from you. However, to accomplish this, you must first know what you want to say. You should always know the 'why' for what you want to say so that you can plan your message and make it as effective as possible. You are wasting your own time if you do not even know what and why you want to influence other people, and they will also not respond well. Sometimes the reason why you want something to happen is obvious, but some cases might require some analyzation. You should take time before your interactions with others to make sure that you are serious and know the reasons why you want to influence. If you are not absolutely certain, you will not be successful.

The last tip for improving your speaking and communication to be more concise is to stay focused. Your undivided attention should be on your interaction and the goals you want to achieve from it. You already know the 'why' for trying to influence someone to do something, and you must keep that in mind. Be sure to not get distracted as you speak and start to go off on an unnecessary tangent. You want people to take you seriously, so you must be serious about it as well.

Once you have reviewed the information in this chapter, you will become a more effective speaker. You also now understand the importance of good communication so that others will listen to you and do what it is that you want. Influencing others becomes much easier when your communication skills are strong.

The more you explore how to improve communication, the more you can influence others. This may be an obvious change you can make, but there are also less obvious changes as well. In the following chapter, we will explore one of these less obvious changes, which is to ask others for favors.

Chapter 4: Ask for Favors

Influencing people will require you to be somewhat manipulative when talking. While manipulating might not be the most ethical way to go about getting what you want, it can prove to be advantageous overall. You can also go about it a positive way.

Manipulation can be done in a variety of ways, some better than others. One of those ways, which is also one of the most effective, is to ask people for favors.

It might sound counterintuitive, but asking for favors makes people perceive you more positively. It even makes you seem like a more influential person. This is a phenomenon called the "Ben Franklin Effect."

Essentially, this effect is described as when a person does a favor for someone else, they become more likely to do more favors for that same person in the future. The thought behind this is that we internalize helping out the other person was because we like them already. This makes sense because we tend to only do extra favors for those that we like, whereas we would not be as willing to do the same for someone we dislike.

This effect is useful in a variety of situations. Imagine being in a business setting where you are trying to get a client to purchase your product. Instead of offering your own assistance to this client, you can ask them to do something for you. For example, you can ask them to tell you their opinion on where the market is heading and what exactly they would want from an ideal product. With this favor going unrepaid, they are likely to do more for you in the future. They will be more likely to give you their time and investments, possibly even purchasing the product from you.

Another term for a similar effect is the "foot in the door" technique. This one is described as asking someone to do a somewhat small favor for you so that they are more willing to do a large favor for you in the future. This one is attributed to what social scientists refer to as "successive approximations."

When a person does a lot of small favors for you, they notice a behavior or attitude change in you that is typically positive. To stop this from turning negative, they will agree to do larger favors for you after doing multiple small ones so that they do not let you down. This is a common business technique but can be used in your own life. If a salesperson comes knocking on your door and asks if you would allow them to come inside, this is likely just the first in a long succession of favors that will be asked of you.

These effects only emphasize the importance of Chapter 2, which describes how to get people to like you. That initial familiarity will be important and will almost guarantee that the other person will agree to that initial, small request.

It may seem weird that people actually enjoy doing favors for one another. We enjoy helping out the people we like, you just need to know the right way to go about asking someone to do something for you.

While you may now understand why asking for a small favor and then a big favor helps you to get what you want, you should also know how to go about asking for these favors. It can be a little awkward to ask people for something, especially if you have tried to avoid doing so in the past. You may be uncomfortable with the idea, but there are appropriate ways to approach people that will help you ease into it.

To go about asking for a favor, you can start by planning to do it at the right time. You want to be courteous to the person you are asking the favor of, as you want to make it seem as tiny of an inconvenience as possible for them. If the timing is wrong, they may be unable or annoyed that you requested anything. Try to find the best time to do so and in the right setting. You do not want to ask a professor to help you with an assignment in the middle of a lecture, and you do not want to ask a friend to borrow something of theirs when you are out with a group of friends. Avoid putting the person in an awkward situation so that they are open to helping you out, no matter what the favor may be.

While asking for a favor should be considerate, you also do not want to state that you are bothering someone by asking them. This immediately looks bad on you and enables the other person to have full control of the situation. It is not bothersome to ask a favor of someone, as we already covered how people actually enjoy doing favors and get pleasure from it.

You also do not want to be sneaky about your intentions when asking for something. It is courteous to let the other person know that you are seeking a favor right away, that way they do not have to figure out what you are trying to get from them. It prepares the other person to consider your request, instead of being surprised by it later. You are also more likely to be rejected if you ask after a long conversation that was leading up to the question. It is best to start off by saying you are looking for a favor and then just asking!

The wording of your request will be vital to success as well. You want to be careful with how you pitch your request, being sure that it is polite and gracious to the other person. After all, they are the one helping you out, so you do not want to be perceived as rude. You also do not want to create any confusion or misunderstandings, so you want to word your request as simple as possible. An example of a simple and polite request would be, "Do you mind sparing about an hour of your time to come to my place and help me study for my Spanish exam?" While specific, the previous example is simple and is considerate of the time you will be taking away from the other person.

As mentioned, you do not want to be rude at all to the person you are asking a favor of. You want to be as polite as possible during the encounter. One way you can go about doing this is to flatter them a little. You do not want to compliment them excessively or to exaggerate their skills, as they can easily see through this. For example, do not tell someone you are seeking their help because they are the best at Algebra, especially if it is not something that they actually excel in. Instead, you can just say that you want their help because you know they are good at it and that you can stand to learn from someone like them. You should also thank them to show your appreciation. Even if they decline to assist you, thanking them shows that you still respect their decision either way. This may also help you in the future if you ask them for help again, as they will be more likely to accept given how polite you were this time.

Along with flattery and being thankful, you also want to make sure that you follow through on any commitments you have made with your requests. For example, if you asked to borrow an item and gave a time frame for returning it, you need to follow through. Getting the item back promptly shows the other person respect and makes them trust you more in the future.

One of the last things to know about asking favors is to offer a way out for the other person. As much as you want the other person to accept your favor, you need to know how to accept a no. You also need to make it possible for them to decline so that they do not feel pressured to accept something they do not want to do. Be sure to note your understanding at the end of your request if they choose to not do whatever you are asking. Also make sure to mention that it is alright if they feel uncomfortable or are unable to accept your request, as this will put them at ease. No one enjoys doing a favor that they feel like they were forced to do, and they will surely not want to do more for you in the future. If you have to force someone into doing something for you, you do not have true influence. It is not hard to gain actual power, at least not compared to the influential power that you can gain over people with skill.

Giving is often more fulfilling than receiving, which is why people are so willing to help each other out. Even if you struggle to get others to do things for you now, this is a skill that you can practice to manipulate others.

When people already like you, it is easy to get them to do favors for you. From there it is all about how you approach the situation and what methods you use to ask. Do not be afraid of asking others for something, as you can get what you want.

You can also get what you want by building your relationships with other people. Sometimes it is not enough for them to just like you and it may require a special emotional connection. We will discuss the best way to go about building this kind of connection in the following chapter.

Chapter 5: Make Emotional Connections

The focus of this chapter is on the emotional connections you make with people to impact them and influence. We have briefly covered this topic before, but this chapter will give you more insight as to how you should build connections and why it is important in influencing other people.

When you are trying to influence others, you may be delivering sensitive or important information to get people to want to do it. This can be an advantage point though, as you should build an emotional connection with the people you are interacting with. This goes hand in hand with making people like you but takes it a little further.

There is a lot of psychological background to this step that suggests its credibility, much of which was researched by John Medina. It has been shown that people 'tune out' of conversations after just a few short minutes and do not retain information if it was boring and uninteresting. To avoid this, you have to build connections with people and make them interested in what you have to say. The way to do this is to get the chemical called dopamine pumping through the person you are interacting with. This chemical is what allows us to feel pleasure and enjoy being around other people. If you can stimulate this part of the brain, you can gain power over others to influence them.

If you want people to listen to you and want to build meaningful connections with them, you will need to start your conversations off strong. You want to grab the attention of the other person and immediately make them feel wanted and important. One of the best ways to do this is to start off with a question or comment that involves the other person. For example, you might start off by asking, "How was your day?" or "What was the most interesting part of your day?" You want the other person to feel as special as possible and grab their attention. When they recognize that you care about them, they will instantly feel more connected and ready to listen.

Another way to build an emotional connection with someone to influence them is to involve them as much as you can in the conversation. You should ask questions and gain the perspective of the other person on what you are discussing. You can also try to analyze their feelings and judge how willing they are to do what it is that you are wanting. Asking questions also makes the other person feel understood and listened to. You should show the other person recognition and show that their thoughts are being considered as well. By doing this, they will like being around you more and will begin to feel much more appreciated. When others feel important, they will be easily influenced.

All of that which has been said thus far is to help you build rapport with the people you want to influence. This is vital to your success, as this connection will make them more likely to do tasks for you. Do not be afraid to get these people talking about themselves. Be sure that you are listening as they talk and are engaging them as much as possible. Learn about these people at any opportunity that is given to you so that you can make comments about their interests along the way. You want to make sure that you make them feel special and that you care about what they do. If you want people to respect and be impacted by you, they must feel a connection.

Another simple way to build emotional connections is to remember the other person's name. This is a small, yet important detail when trying to influence someone. While it may not seem like much when you remember a name, not remembering can have many negative effects that will be hard to come back from. You want to be able to say the other person's name regularly so that they feel validated and remembered. By not remembering, the other person senses that you do not truly care and that you cannot even remember the small things about them. If this is the perception that they have, then they will likely not do anything for you.

We have already covered the importance of being positive around others to get them to do what you want, but you should also look for the positives in them. It is a natural tendency to be somewhat cynical and not immediately see the good in people, but there is plenty of good to look for. If you want to be successful in building emotional connections, you will need to master looking for this. Be sure to focus on reasons to like them and set aside any reasons you may not want to be around them. This will help you to expect the best out of people, which they will then deliver once the connections are made.

When trying to make emotional connections with people, you expect them to open up to you a bit. This is how you will build trust with them and make the connections real. It is important that they open up to you and do not regret it later on. You want to avoid mocking or making the other person feel judged, thus regretting showing that side of them to you. If this happens, it is highly unlikely that they will be strongly influenced by you anymore and they may try to even do the opposite of whatever you say. Instead, you should try to empathize with them and their beliefs. Even if you do not agree with what they do, empathy can show that you respect their decisions to do something a certain way and even gives you the chance to reveal more about yourself. You want to be open and non-judgmental so that people trust you and are not afraid to be themselves around you. Without this quality, people will not listen to you or be influenced by what you say.

Getting a little personal will also help you to build a connection with others. We have already stated that you should ask questions to try to get to know someone, but do not be afraid to dig a little deeper than superficial questions. When someone tells you what they do for a living, try to ask why they chose that profession or what made them want to do that. This will help them open up to you and reveal more about themselves that you might not have otherwise known. You can learn what they care about and what makes them tick. This will also give you the chance to show your passions so that there is mutual respect, which will then give you the opportunity to have a higher impact on them later on.

Along with everything else you do to connect to people, the most important thing that you can do is to treat people the way that you would want to be treated. This is the 'golden rule' for being nice to others, one that you may have been taught from a young age. You will show a lot of deserved respect to the other person when you follow this rule, as no one wishes to be treated poorly. You will also find that you want to listen to them even more and gain their insight, such as you would if the tables were turned.

It is also worth mentioning that you should not try to 'one-up' someone when building connections and friendships with them. As people tell you about themselves, be sure to not use it as an opportunity to brag about yourself and your accomplishments. While self-disclosure is necessary and assists in building relationships, you do not want to overdo it. The point is to influence other people and learn about them. If you are too focused on yourself, all of your other attempts will have been for nothing. Make sure you are taking time to listen and build the connection effectively and without selfish causes.

Influencing others will require you to connect with others and build strong relationships with them. We listen to the people that we respect the most and feel comfortable with. You should utilize this fact to your own advantage so that you gain power over people and can have an impact on them. You want people to perceive you as approachable so that they can come to you with requests, which you can then ask for in return later on.

There are many advantages to connecting with other people, the most obvious one being the power that it gives you to them. By reading the information in this chapter, you are well prepared to start improving your connections with people and use them to influence as you want.

In the next chapter you will learn how to use your connections that you have built and to become more transparent to other people. This will provide you even more power to influence others and to have an impact on the lives of others.

Chapter 6: Be More Transparent

To be persuasive and get people to do what you want, you need to be vulnerable and make your intentions clear. We touched upon this topic when learning how to ask for a favor, as you want to make it apparent what you want right away.

You may wonder why you should be transparent about your intentions when trying to get what you want from others. Doesn't this take away from the manipulative aspect of influencing? Maybe so, but being transparent actually helps to get other people to do what you want. Being open and vulnerable increases your likability, and therefore your influence. People like to see your emotions, and they will also trust you more when doing so. Most people assume you would not show them your vulnerable side if you did not like or trust them in return.

Being transparent also means being able to admit your mistakes. Admitting to your own flaws and weaknesses shows the other person that you are 'real' and are an equivalent to them. They can relate to you on a more personal level when you display emotions and admit to your weaknesses. This will get them to trust and like you even more, thus resulting in a higher ability to influence on your end. You do not want to make yourself seem perfect out of fear that others will think less of you. We are all only human, and we all know that each person messes up from time to time, so do not be afraid to own up to this fact.

To start being more transparent, remember to make your intentions obvious from the start. If you plan on asking someone something, let them know immediately. If you just want to talk to that person and spend time with them, make this obvious as well. Do not leave your audience guessing what it is that you want, as this decreases their willingness to give it to you.

You also need to learn how to be open with others. This does not mean you have to reveal every intricate detail of your life, but you should not be afraid to open up. You want people to be able to read you so that they trust you and everything that you say. Think about what others might find interesting to know about you and tell them! You would be surprised at the connections this will help you build and how much others will respect how vulnerable you make yourself.

To be open with others, you should tell a story about yourself that demonstrates what kind of person you are. You might select a funny story or a vignette about your day that gives them a snapshot of your life. No matter what instance you choose, you want it to reflect who you are. It does not hurt to add something in that makes the other person smile, as well as something to personalize the story that shows your character. The purpose of this is to tell the other person more about yourself, so be as detailed as necessary. Of course, you should only use this tip if the timing is right and if it is warranted. You will need to be your own judge of this, but do not be afraid to utilize this helpful strategy.

Being transparent can also involve sharing your thoughts and opinions on topics, even if they are controversial. You do not want to bite your tongue all of the time if you desire to be impactful. You should know your stance on a subject and be able to back it up. People will respect that you know your stance and are well-educated enough to discuss it openly. Even if you do not think others will agree with you, it is ok to share your thoughts on a subject. You should still be respectful of other people's opinions and not think less of them if they disagree with you. This allows people to see your way of thinking and get an idea of how your mind works.

You can also be more transparent by keeping people in the loop about your life. When people like you, they will take a genuine interest in your life, and you should be willing to let them know more about yourself. For example, if you have been working on a blog or searching for a new job, other people might be interested to know this about you. This makes it easy for other people to engage you in conversation and find out more. They may also be more likely to get involved with what you are doing and want to take part in it, which may be a potential benefit to you as well.

One of the most obvious, yet often overlooked, aspects of transparency is honesty. While what we have covered so far implies that making yourself vulnerable involves being honest about yourself with others, it does not hurt to remind yourself of this as well. You do not want to hide who you are from other people, as they will never trust you. Do not be afraid to share your honest opinions and thoughts, even when others do not agree. You will be more successful in earning respect by sharing what you think without trying to cover it up anyway. This can be scary for some people, as we often put a filter on ourselves to avoid judgment. As long as you approach each situation the right way and create an environment of mutual respect, you should have no problem being honest to become more transparent.

Along with being honest, you should also take care not to give people a false sense of hope or provide pretenses. This is a part of being honest, but can still be a cause of a misunderstanding. Sometimes just the tone of voice or way you approach a situation can give people the wrong idea and make them expect something that might not be guaranteed. For example, if you are a boss at your company and you always approach one of your employees in a cautious, friendly manner, they might not realize when an issue has become serious. Even if you have redirected them in the past, the way you approached the situation might have been misleading for them. Do not assume that people will always understand your meaning, as this can cause miscommunication. Instead, be honest and upfront about everything. Do not try to "sugarcoat" anything, especially not when it is something important. You want people to be able to not only hear but also to see your intentions, no matter what the situation is.

When being transparent, you should take caution not to come off as self-centered. Of course, this step requires you to talk about yourself, but you must know the limits. Do not spend the entire conversation talking about yourself and your own emotions. Be sure to involve the other person and ask questions about them as well, just as you learned from previous steps. Even if they are not being as transparent about themselves as you are, it is good to offer them the opportunity to share after you have revealed more about yourself.

Transparency and vulnerability will assist you in your endeavors to be influential. These are the qualities you need to get people to listen and care about what you say, as they show that you have absolutely nothing to hide. This is a technique that the greatest of leaders use to get people to trust them and to make their disciples like them. Transparency and vulnerability also have the benefit of improving your friendships and relationships, as these traits are appreciated by just about everyone you will meet.

People will also feel more connected to you when you make yourself vulnerable to them. As we have covered before, this feeling of closeness will make them more likely to do what you want, which has been the overall goal for each of these steps.

In the next chapter, we will cover how to take an interest in others to gain influence, as this chapter has mostly revolved around getting people to know more about you. These steps, in combination with everything else that has been covered, will get you much closer to being an influential person.

Chapter 7: Take an Interest in Others

A lot of this book has focused on working with others. After all, you can only influence people that are willing to listen to you. This chapter will reiterate this important fact and help you to work even better with other people.

People want to feel liked and respected, as we have discovered. It cannot be underestimated how being nice to others will get you what you want. Part of being nice to others will also require you to take an interest in others.

We already know that we should ask questions and pay full attention when other people are talking to us. You can also do a lot to show that you are attentive and listening, such as making appropriate eye contact.

Along with what has been covered so far, there are many other ways that you can show your interest in others. One of these ways is to learn how to read people.

Every person has different qualities and practices that will be influenced in different ways. It will be your job to figure out how each person works so that you can read what will work on them.

To read people, you should start by paying attention to their body, both language, and characteristics. This will indicate a lot about their current emotions and will tell you what they are feeling. For example, if the person has their arms crossed and looks away from you, they are probably not in a great mood. You might also notice any tattoos they have or a special ring that they are wearing that you might comment on. You can learn a lot about a person just based on what they wear and how they carry themselves, so be sure to note these things when interacting with someone.

Reading people will also involve paying attention to the emotions that they are trying to show you. While some of this is readable from body language and appearance, you will also be able to sense emotions. Intuition will be used to understand what other people are feeling, and you should be sure to consider this and obvious signs that they are conveying. For example, when you meet someone, you should think about how they are making you feel. Do you feel delighted to be around them or do you feel somewhat uncomfortable? How you feel is often based on the vibe that the other person is giving off, which might be responded to by your subconscious mind. You should also pay attention to their tone of voice and laughter as they are talking, which will convey their emotions. You may notice that some people get a higher pitched voice when they are nervous or that their voice tends to shake around certain topics. Making note of this is important because you will be able to tell what they are feeling based on these sounds.

When trying to read someone you should also notice the spacial differences between the two of you. You can tell if someone is interested in talking to you based on how far away they sit or stand. The person may not necessarily have something against you personally even if they are standing far away, but it does give you an indication that something is not right. It could be that they do not want to feel intimate or vulnerable at that time, or perhaps they are more of an introverted person in general and do not want to be close physically.

By learning how to read others, you take an interest in what they are feeling and how they act around you. You can also show your interest by offering compliments to the people you talk to. Not only does this make them feel good about themselves, they recognize that you pay attention to them. It is best if the compliments that you give are based on qualities or characteristics you have learned about a person from talking to them. An example might be that they have mentioned to you that they planned on going to the gym more often. You could use this as an opportunity the next time you speak to notice that their arms look more toned than before. Your compliments should be genuine, as this is what will make people feel the best and will make them realize that you do care.

You should also be sure to remember special occasions and events that people have going on in their lives. If they tell you that they are going on a vacation or that their brother is getting married, you can remember these dates to bring them up later. It makes people feel special when you remember details about their lives, so do not just pass over them. They also did not mention them to you to be forgotten, and many people want you to remember what is going on in their life. When you make people feel remembered and show you have an interest in them, they can be easily influenced.

Showing interest in others can also be as simple as starting a conversation with them. Do not be afraid to follow up with someone after talking to them and do not show fear of being the first one to reach out. You need to make it clear that you want to know more about that person and that you care about your connection with them. Some people are afraid of being the first to contact the other, but you show power and courage in doing so.

You should also give well-thought-out feedback to people to show your interest. This is accomplished somewhat by complimenting but is not always the same. Providing feedback offers your general thoughts on something, as opposed to just the positive opinions or observations you have. You need to think about what other people tell you and judge when they want your opinion on something. People often seek approval or guidance from the people they trust, so it is a good sign if you are at this point with them. Be honest with them about your thoughts on each matter, but know your limits as well. Many people respect honesty, but you do not want to be so blunt that you hurt their feelings. Your feedback needs to be both considerate and honest so that the other person is appreciative instead of defensive.

Taking an interest in people mostly involves the respect that you show others. Everything we have learned in this chapter is what you should already be doing, but may be missing in your current interactions.

If you want to have an impact on what people do, you need to make an impact on their emotions first. No one will listen to you if you mean very little to them or do not show any interest in their lives. The point of this chapter is to help you show others that you do care and that you listen to their desires and what is going on in their lives.

Hopefully, by now, you have identified a few ways to go about showing an interest in other people, as well as the many other ways to involve people and their lives. All of this will help you to influence them because they will pick up on the efforts that you have shown them.

Chapter 8: Summary of Steps

This book has covered the seven most important steps to learning how to influence people. To be successful, it is important that you re-read these steps as needed and practice them often.

This chapter is meant to serve as a quick guide for you. Each step will be covered and given a small summary for your benefit.

Step 1: Having confident body language. This first step is meant to help you look the part and be confident.

Start by keeping your head, push out your chest, pull your stomach in, and keep your shoulders back. Monitor any non-purposeful movements you might be doing and maintain eye contact.

Body language is the first impression you give someone, so be sure that this step is always one of the first things you consider when trying to be influential.

Step 2: Make people like you. This step sounds easy enough, and you might already be good at accomplishing this.

If you need some help with making people like you, do not worry. You can start by being more charismatic. Do not be afraid to take control in a room and show that you care. People will respect you and enjoy being around you. It also will not hurt to make a joke every now and then as well.

Being humble will also start to make others like you, so do not forget to show humility now and again.

Step 3: Be clear and concise. You want people to understand your message and take out any guesswork.

Articulate what you want to say by taking out long, complicated words and get straight to the point. Make sure you use as many active verbs as possible and do not use vague nouns and words to send a message or ask a favor.

You also want to consider what you are going to say before you say it. This will help to make your message more concise after you have simplified it. You should also be sure to start and end with the main point. Keep supporting details to a minimum and include them in the middle of your overall message.

Step 4: Ask for favors. Use the principles of the "Ben Franklin Effect" to get people to do what you ask of them.

By getting people to agree to do small favors for you, you can also get them to do larger favors for you afterward.

You can also get people to do what you want by asking for it in an appropriate way. Be considerate of the other person and plan to ask at a time that works for them. You also want to be polite and make your intentions clear.

Do not be afraid to ask a favor of someone, but also be prepared for them to decline your favor.

Step 5: Make emotional connections. Sometimes it is not enough to have people like you to get them to do what you want. You need to work on building meaningful relationships with them, especially if you want long-lasting success in having influence over them.

You can do this by having strong conversations with people and by building rapport with them. You want them to talk about themselves and their experiences so that you can learn more about them. Once you know a lot about them, you can bring up what is going on in their life and show that you have been paying attention to what they have told you.

Step 6: Be more transparent. You want people to know who you are and not have to guess about your life. Do not be afraid to share about yourself or any emotions you have.

Being transparent will require you to be more vulnerable and open up to people. You want to be honest with them and show that they can trust you. They will also feel like they know you much better, which will be an important factor in getting them to listen to you.

Step 7: Take an interest in others. Do not be afraid to get to know people and pay attention to their lives. People love to feel special and as though you care about what they say.

Give compliments and feedback to people when warranted. Do not be afraid to reach out to them to talk or meet up, as this shows that you care. You want people to feel remembered, and showing an interest in their lives will accomplish this.

If you feel like you have missed any part of these steps, feel free to go back and read the chapter again. Each suggestion and tip can bring you closer to getting people to listen to you, so it is important that you understand each concept well.

Once you have reviewed each step, you are ready to do it on your own. Good luck and enjoy your newly found influence over others!

Conclusion

Thank you for making it through to the end of this book, let's hope it was informative and able to provide you with all of the tools you need to achieve your goals, whatever they may be.

The next step is to put the 7 steps into practice so that you may begin to influence the people around you. By learning and practicing each of the steps given in this book you will easily gain control over others and can make them do just about anything you want.

You have learned new skills, such as improving body language and how to make emotional connections, so that you can influence other people. It is now up to you to demonstrate your learned skills and get people to do what you want. This is no easy task, but soon you will be a professional at getting others to do your bidding.

Yes, it takes a lot of practice to master the different ways to influence people. You will find being able to influence – and manipulate – others can be very beneficial especially if you are someone that needs to show dominance over others. Of course, how you want to influence others will completely depend on you. You can be someone with positive influence to your peers or you can be someone who's very manipulative to others.

Finally, if you found this book useful in any way, your honest review on Amazon is always appreciated.

More by Dean Mack

Discover all books from the Social Skills Best Seller Series by Dean Mack at:

bit.ly/dean-mack

Book 1: *How to Flirt*

Book 2: *How to Start a Conversation*

Book 3: *How to Talk to People*

Book 4: *How to Ask Questions*

Book 5: *How to Be Funny*

Book 6: *How to Influence People*

Book 7: *How to Attract Men*

Book 8: *How to Attract Women*

Themed book bundles available at discounted prices:

bit.ly/dean-mack